FOR THIS REASON

God's Word in 90 Days

⨠

Darrelyn L. Tutt

Copyright © 2012
Tutt Darrelyn L.
All Rights Reserved

All rights reserved. No part of this book may be reproduced in any form, except for the inclusion of brief quotations in a review, without permission in writing from the author or publisher.

Library of Congress Control Number: 2012916168

ISBN: 978-0-9768567-1-9

First Printing   November 2012

Additional copies of this book are available at:
www.El-Inkwell.com

Scripture references are taken from the King James Version (KJV).

Printed in the United States by Morris Publishing®
3212 East Highway 30
Kearney, NE 68847
1-800-650-7888

Dedication

to Joshua, Hannah, and Jessica

I have no greater joy than to hear
that my children walk in truth.

—3 John 4

Acknowledgments

I wish to acknowledge...

Scot Tutt

You're a margin setter in my life. You contribute quiet, solid settings to my character, life, and writing. How gratifying it is to celebrate a completed work with you.

Dave Harthan

Your character and intellect are thought-provoking and inspiring. This book is a testament to what you've contributed to my life.

Kathy Shaibani

Your editing skills and eye for detail are remarkable. Thank you for contributing to the clarity contained in this book.

Reading Schedule
Month 1

DAY 1	Genesis 1–12; Psalms 1 and 2; Proverbs 1	8
DAY 2	Genesis 13–25; Psalms 3 and 4; Proverbs 2	10
DAY 3	Genesis 26–38; Psalms 5 and 6; Proverbs 3	12
DAY 4	Genesis 39–50; Psalms 7 and 8; Proverbs 4	14
DAY 5	Exodus 1–12; Psalms 9 and 10; Proverbs 5	16
DAY 6	Exodus 13–25; Psalms 11 and 12; Proverbs 6	18
DAY 7	Exodus 26–40; Psalms 13 and 14; Proverbs 7	20
DAY 8	Leviticus 1–13; Psalms 15 and 16; Proverbs 8	22
DAY 9	Leviticus 14–27; Psalms 17 and 18; Proverbs 9	24
DAY 10	Numbers 1–12; Psalms 19 and 20; Proverbs 10	26
DAY 11	Numbers 13–26; Psalms 21 and 22; Proverbs 11	28
DAY 12	Numbers 27–36; Psalms 23 and 24; Proverbs 12	30
DAY 13	Deuteronomy 1–12; Psalms 25 and 26; Proverbs 13	32
DAY 14	Deuteronomy 13–23; Psalm 27 and 28; Proverbs 14	34
DAY 15	Deuteronomy 24–34; Psalm 29 and 30; Proverbs 15	36
DAY 16	Galatians 1–6; Psalm 31 and 32; Proverbs 16	38
DAY 17	Joshua 1–12; Psalm 33 and 34; Proverbs 17	40
DAY 18	Joshua 13–24; Psalm 35 and 36; Proverbs 18	42
DAY 19	Judges 1–12; Psalm 37 and 38; Proverbs 19	44
DAY 20	Judges 13–21; Psalm 39 and 40; Proverbs 20	46
DAY 21	Ruth 1–4; Psalms 41 and 42; Proverbs 21	48
DAY 22	1 Samuel 1–15; Psalm 43 and 44; Proverbs 22	50
DAY 23	1 Samuel 16–31; Psalm 45 and 46; Proverbs 23	52
DAY 24	2 Samuel 1–12; Psalm 47 and 48; Proverbs 24	54
DAY 25	2 Samuel 13–24; Psalm 49 and 50; Proverbs 25	56
DAY 26	Ephesians 1–6; Psalm 51 and 52; Proverbs 26	58
DAY 27	1 Kings 1–11; Psalm 53 and 54; Proverbs 27	60
DAY 28	1 Kings 12–22; Psalm 55 and 56; Proverbs 28	62
DAY 29	2 Kings 1–12; Psalm 57–58; Proverbs 29	64
DAY 30	2 Kings 13–25; Psalm 59–60; Proverbs 30	66

Month 2

DAY 31	Philippians 1–4; Psalm 61–62; Proverbs 31	68
DAY 32	1 Chronicles 1–15; Psalm 63–64	70
DAY 33	1 Chronicles 16–29; Psalm 65–66	72
DAY 34	2 Chronicles 1–12; Psalm 67–68	74
DAY 35	2 Chronicles 13–25; Psalm 69–70	76
DAY 36	2 Chronicles 26–36; Psalm 71–72	78
DAY 37	Colossians 1-4; Psalm 73-74	80
DAY 38	Ezra 1–10; Psalm 75–76	82
DAY 39	Nehemiah 1–13; Psalm 77–78	84
DAY 40	Esther 1–10; Psalm 79–80	86
DAY 41	Job 1–14; Psalm 81–82	88
DAY 42	Job 15–28; Psalm 83–84	90
DAY 43	Job 29–42; Psalm 85–86	92
DAY 44	Ecclesiastes 1–12; Psalm 87–88	94
DAY 45	Song of Solomon 1–8; Psalm 89–90	96
DAY 46	Isaiah 1–14; Psalm 91–92	98
DAY 47	Isaiah 15–26; Psalm 93–94	100
DAY 48	Isaiah 27–40; Psalm 95–96	102
DAY 49	Isaiah 41–53; Psalm 97–98	104
DAY 50	Isaiah 54–66; Psalm 99–100	106
DAY 51	Matthew 1–14; Psalm 101–102	108
DAY 52	Matthew 15–28; Psalm 103–104	110
DAY 53	Jeremiah 1–13; Psalm 105–106	112
DAY 54	Jeremiah 14–28; Psalm 107–108	114
DAY 55	Jeremiah 29–41; Psalm 109–110	116
DAY 56	Jeremiah 42–52; Psalm 111–112	118
DAY 57	Lamentations 1–5; Psalm 113–114	120
DAY 58	Mark 1–8; Psalm 115–116	122
DAY 59	Mark 9–16; Psalm 117–118	124
DAY 60	Ezekiel 1–12; Psalm 119:1–40	126

Month 3

DAY 61	Ezekiel 13–24; Psalm 119:41–80	128
DAY 62	Ezekiel 25–36; Psalm 119:81–120	130
DAY 63	Ezekiel 37–48; Psalm 119:121–150	132
DAY 64	Luke 1–12; Psalm 119:151–176	134
DAY 65	Luke 13–24; Psalm 120–121	136
DAY 66	Daniel 1–12; Psalm 122–123	138
DAY 67	John 1–10; Psalm 124–125	140
DAY 68	John 11–21; Psalm 126–127	142
DAY 69	Hosea 1–14; Psalm 128–129	144
DAY 70	Acts 1–14; Psalm 130	146
DAY 71	Acts 15–28; Psalm 131	148
DAY 72	Joel 1–3; Psalm 132	150
DAY 73	Amos 1–9; Obadiah; Psalm 133	152
DAY 74	Romans 1–8; Psalm 134	154
DAY 75	Romans 9–16; Psalm 135	156
DAY 76	Jonah 1–4; Micah 1–7; Psalm 136	158
DAY 77	1 Corinthians 1–8; Psalm 137	160
DAY 78	1 Corinthians 9–16; Psalm 138	162
DAY 79	2 Corinthians 1–13; Psalm 139	164
DAY 80	Nahum 1–3; Habakkuk 1–3; Zephaniah 1–3; Haggai 1–2; Psalm 140	166
DAY 81	1 Thessalonians 1–5; 2 Thessalonians 1–3; Psalm 141	168
DAY 82	Zechariah 1–14; Psalm 142	170
DAY 83	Malachi 1–4; Psalm 143	172
DAY 84	1 Timothy 1–6; 2 Timothy 1–4; Psalm 144	174
DAY 85	Titus 1–3; Philemon; Psalm 145	176
DAY 86	Hebrews 1–13; Psalm 146	178
DAY 87	James 1–5; 1 Peter 1–5; 2 Peter 1–3; Psalm 147	180
DAY 88	1 John 1–5; 2 John; 3 John; Jude; Psalm 148	182
DAY 89	Revelation 1–11; Psalm 149	184
DAY 90	Revelation 12–22; Psalm 150	186

Introduction

For this reason also, since the day we heard of it, we have not ceased to pray for you and to ask that you may be filled with the knowledge of His will in all spiritual wisdom and understanding.

—Colossians 1:9 (NASB)

Several years ago, I was challenged by a godly individual to read through the Bible in 90 days. Like a long distance runner approaching a first marathon, I eagerly took hold of the challenge. Plunging into the Word with an earnest heart, I sought the Lord with *all* of me, and since trying this approach I have never tired of reading through the Word in this fashion. It's become an integral and consistent part of my spiritual journey and has never ceased to bless me.

In posing the 90-day challenge to others, I have discovered that men and women alike are hungry for spiritual challenge and for more of God's Word. Whether you read Scripture alone, with an accountability partner, or with a group, you will be blessed. I have used a variety of reading partners, schedules, and Bible versions and have discovered a certain "reader's high" every time I pass through. The Word is just plain good. I encourage you to get into it!

A few practical points before you begin:

- The reading format was developed with the first-time reader in mind and has been designed strategically. Each book of the Bible is scheduled as tightly as possible in order to retain the cohesiveness of the book. Heavy reading assignments will give way to lighter ones, giving the reader a much-needed break at intervals. New Testament books have been

integrated constructively into the Old to help the reader grasp how the whole of God's Word is tied together and to help with the digestion of God's Word.
- If you miss a day, don't try to play catch-up. Do that day's reading and keep moving!
- Reading God's Word paves the way to praying God's Word, which becomes one of the most inspiring aspects of the journey. Get personal with God and let His word move and touch your heart in response to Him.

There are countless ways to travel through God's word in 90 days, but I think you'll find the first time around a treasure beyond words. That's what this book is about!

The title of the book is taken from Colossians 1:9 and expresses my heart toward you. God's richest blessing to you as you begin your 90 days.

Yours on the journey,

Darrelyn L. Tutt
Miller, South Dakota

So shall my word be that goeth forth out of my mouth: it shall not return unto me void, but it shall accomplish that which I please, and it shall prosper in the thing whereto I sent it.

—Isaiah 55:11

DAY 1

Scripture: Genesis 1–12; Psalms 1 and 2; Proverbs 1

And Abel, he also brought of the firstlings of his flock and of the fat thereof. And the LORD had respect unto Abel and to his offering.

Genesis 4:4

For the LORD knoweth the way of the righteous: but the way of the ungodly shall perish.

Psalm 1:6

Turn you at my reproof: behold, I will pour out my spirit unto you, I will make known my words unto you.

Proverbs 1:23

*Beloved Father,
I long for You to look on me as You looked on Abel:
with pleasure in what I offer to You.
Help me to hold back nothing from You today
and to love You with openness and joy.
Make straight the path that I should walk
and give me discernment as I interact with others.
Pour out a spirit of wisdom upon me
and make known Your words
unto me. Amen.*

For This Reason

DAY 1

Record one key reference each from your readings in Genesis, Psalms, and Proverbs:

Turn your references into a prayer.

For This Reason

DAY 2

Scripture: Genesis 13–25; Psalms 3 and 4; Proverbs 2

After these things the word of the LORD came unto Abram in a vision, saying, Fear not, Abram: I am thy shield, and thy exceeding great reward.

Genesis 15:1

But thou, O LORD, art a shield for me; my glory, and the lifter up of mine head.

Psalm 3:3

He layeth up sound wisdom for the righteous: He is a buckler to them that walk uprightly.

Proverbs 2:7

Protective Father,
obedience to You involves countless unknowns,
and those unknowns can bring fear.
Abram heard Your voice and responded to You;
he needed Your protection every step of the way.
I do, too. Be a shield for me from the evil that surrounds me; be my glory
and the lifter of my head and countenance. You have laid up wisdom for
me in Your word;
help me to invest wisely in it.
Be my buckler and my exceeding great reward.
Amen.

For This Reason

DAY 2

Record one key reference each from your readings in Genesis, Psalms, and Proverbs:

Turn your references into a prayer.

DAY 3

Scripture: Genesis 26–38; Psalms 5 and 6; Proverbs 3

And Jacob went on his way, and the angels of God met him.

Genesis 32:1

But let all those that put their trust in thee rejoice: let them ever shout for joy, because thou defendest them: let them also that love thy name be joyful in thee.

Psalm 5:11

Trust in the LORD with all thine heart; and lean not unto thine own understanding. In all thy ways acknowledge him, and he shall direct thy paths.

Proverbs 3:5–6

Father, my Provider,
as you went with Jacob, in his fear and trepidation
to meet his brother Esau, so go with me.
I place my trust in You, Lord, confident that it is You
who will defend and rescue me from the one I fear.
Let me rejoice in the knowledge that Your defense over me
is perfect and that what happens to me is ordained and
allowed for my good. I trust in You, lean on You,
and acknowledge You, Lord. Direct my path
and provide for my way.
Amen.

For This Reason

DAY 3

Record one key reference each from your readings in Genesis, Psalms, and Proverbs:

Jacob wrestling w/ God

Proverbs

Do not despise the Lord's discipline, and do not resent His rebuke

Turn your references into a prayer.

DAY 4

Scripture: Genesis 39–50; Psalms 7 and 8; Proverbs 4

But as for you, ye thought evil against me; but God meant it unto good, to bring to pass, as it is this day, to save much people alive.

Genesis 50:20

Oh let the wickedness of the wicked come to an end; but establish the just: for the righteous God trieth the hearts and reins.

Psalm 7:9

But the path of the just is as the shining light, that shineth more and more unto the perfect day.

Proverbs 4:18

*Sustaining Father,
Joseph's life is such an encouragement
to me. He faced mistreatment and injustice,
but Your hand was on him, and You loved
and sustained him. I sense that Your hand
also rests on me, and I give You thanks, Lord.
You will preserve me from every evil and determine
the end of those who devise ill against me.
Enlighten my path and reveal
Your glory through my life. Amen.*

For This Reason

DAY 4

Record one key reference each from your readings
in Genesis, Psalms, and Proverbs:

Turn your references into a prayer.

For This Reason

DAY 5

Scripture: Exodus 1–12; Psalms 9 and 10; Proverbs 5

And the people believed: and when they heard that the Lord had visited the children of Israel, and that he had looked upon their affliction, then they bowed their heads and worshipped.
Exodus 4:31

The Lord also will be a refuge for the oppressed, a refuge in times of trouble.
Psalm 9:9

For the ways of man are before the eyes of the Lord, and he pondereth all his goings.
Proverbs 5:21

*Merciful Father,
Your compassion extends to me in my affliction
just as it did to Your people Israel. Visit me
when I am oppressed and bowed down,
and be the refuge I can run to today.
Give me a heart that worships You,
and help me to recount the countless ways
You have delivered me. Father, look with mercy and
compassion upon my soul, and in my distress
draw me closer to You. You consider my ways,
and I consider Your grace.
Amen.*

For This Reason

DAY 5

Record one key reference each from your readings
in Exodus, Psalms, and Proverbs:

Turn your references into a prayer.

DAY 6

Scripture: Exodus 13–25; Psalms 11 and 12; Proverbs 6

Now therefore, if ye will obey my voice indeed, and keep my covenant, then ye shall be a peculiar treasure unto me above all people: for all the earth is mine…

Exodus 19:5

The words of the LORD are pure words: as silver tried in a furnace of earth, purified seven times.

Psalm 12:6

For the commandment is a lamp; and the law is light; and reproofs of instruction are the way of life…

Proverbs 6:23

Sanctifying Father,
as one of Your people, I have been set apart for
Your glory and Your name's sake. Obedience to Your word
gives my life definition, and I am known and regarded as
peculiar and distinguished. This is what I am in You!
Truly, Your every word is pure, Lord,
as silver tried and purified by fire seven times over.
Your commandments and words are radiant and glorious,
and Your reproofs are a necessary instruction for my life.
Give me an increasing love for the purity of Your word, and
sanctify Your name through me.
Amen.

For This Reason

DAY 6

Record one key reference each from your readings in Exodus, Psalms, and Proverbs:

Turn your references into a prayer.

DAY 7

Scripture: Exodus 26–40; Psalms 13 and 14; Proverbs 7

And the LORD passed by before him, and proclaimed, The LORD, The LORD God, merciful and gracious, longsuffering, and abundant in goodness and truth...
Exodus 34:6

But I have trusted in thy mercy; my heart shall rejoice in thy salvation.
Psalm 13:5

Keep my commandments, and live; and my law as the apple of thine eye.
Proverbs 7:2

Patient Father,
Moses longed to see Your glory and receive
just a glimpse of You with earthly eyes, and
You granted his request. I also desire to see and behold Your glory and
to know You more fully.
Today, afford me a glimpse of Your holiness in some tangible, personal
way. I rejoice in the mercy
You apply to me and the salvation
You grant to me. You are patient in all
Your ways, and Your Word is given to me
that I might live. You are my desire.
Amen.

For This Reason

DAY 7

Record one key reference each from your readings in Exodus, Psalms, and Proverbs:

Turn your references into a prayer.

DAY 8

Scripture: Leviticus 1–13; Psalms 15 and 16; Proverbs 8

For I am the LORD that bringeth you up out of the land of Egypt, to be your God: ye shall therefore be holy, for I am holy.

Leviticus 11:45

I have set the LORD always before me: because he is at my right hand, I shall not be moved.

Psalm 16:8

Blessed is the man that heareth me, watching daily at my gates, waiting at the posts of my doors.

Proverbs 8:34

*Holy Father,
like Israel, You have brought me up out of a
land of slavery for Your great name's sake, and
delivered me from a life of bondage and sin.
You have set Your seal of ownership upon my life
and established me as holy. What a wonder
You are, O God of glory! Your Son is seated at Your right hand,
interceding for me, and I shall not be moved. You are holy.
Impart a spirit of wisdom to me so that I hear You, watch for You, and
wait for You, for only You are holy. Amen.*

For This Reason

DAY 8

Record one key reference each from your readings in Leviticus, Psalms, and Proverbs:

Turn your references into a prayer.

DAY 9

Scripture: Leviticus 14–27; Psalms 17 and 18; Proverbs 9

And ye shall be holy unto me: for I the Lord am holy, and have severed you from other people, that ye should be mine.

Leviticus 20:26

Thou hast delivered me from the strivings of the people; and thou hast made me the head of the heathen: a people whom I have not known shall serve me.

Psalm 18:43

Forsake the foolish, and live; and go in the way of understanding.

Proverbs 9:6

*Sovereign Father,
separation is a theme for all those You redeem.
Just as You set Israel apart, so have You graciously
called and set me apart. I am holy because You are holy, and You have
granted a glorious position
to my feeble frame. What a marvel! Deliver me
from evil foes and forces, and set me apart
for a noble and exalted purpose.
Forsaking the world, I follow
a sovereign Savior.
Amen.*

For This Reason

DAY 9

Record one key reference each from your readings
in Leviticus, Psalms, and Proverbs:

Turn your references into a prayer.

For This Reason

DAY 10

Scripture: Numbers 1–12; Psalms 19 and 20; Proverbs 10

And when the people complained, it displeased the LORD: and the LORD heard it; and his anger was kindled…

Numbers 11:1

Let the words of my mouth, and the meditation of my heart, be acceptable in thy sight, O LORD, my strength, and my redeemer.

Psalm 19:14

The lips of the righteous feed many: but fools die for want of wisdom.

Proverbs 10:21

*Heavenly Father,
how often I complain, murmur, and
utter words that display a faithless and evil heart.
Your anger is kindled toward me when I speak
the way Israel did, and when I am not thankful.
Forgive me, Lord, and cause the words of
my mouth and the meditation of
my heart to be acceptable and pleasing
in Your sight. Cause my words to be few,
chosen before spoken,
and worthy of praise.
Amen.*

For This Reason

DAY 10

Record one key reference each from your readings in Numbers, Psalms, and Proverbs.

Turn your references into a prayer.

For This Reason

DAY 11

Scripture: Numbers 13–26; Psalms 21 and 22; Proverbs 11

Thus Edom refused to give Israel passage through his border: wherefore Israel turned away from him.

Numbers 20:21

O my God, I cry in the day time, but thou hearest not; and in the night season, and am not silent.

Psalm 22:2

Though hand join in hand, the wicked shall not be unpunished: but the seed of the righteous shall be delivered.

Proverbs 11:21

Attentive Father,
Edom refused to give Israel passage through
their land and discouraged them much on the way.
In the same way, I have people in my life whose
favor I do not procure, and I am disheartened by their
intention to discourage me. Lord, I cry out to You,
knowing that You see all of these distresses in my soul.
Do not be silent. Deliver me from the "Edoms,"
and preserve my way.
Amen.

For This Reason

DAY 11

Record one key reference each from your readings in Numbers, Psalms, and Proverbs:

Turn your references into a prayer.

DAY 12

Scripture: Numbers 27–36; Psalms 23 and 24; Proverbs 12

And the LORD said unto Moses, Take thee Joshua the son of Nun, a man in whom is the Spirit, and lay thine hand upon him...

Numbers 27:18

He that hath clean hands, and a pure heart; who hath not lifted up his soul unto vanity, nor sworn deceitfully. He shall receive the blessing from the LORD, and righteousness from the God of his salvation.

Psalm 24:4–5

The hand of the diligent shall bear rule: but the slothful shall be under tribute.

Proverbs 12:24

Discerning Father,
let me be a wise and Spirit-filled leader,
as Joshua was. Cause me to be devoted to
Your name, and let me be a faithful witness
of Your glory. Grant me clean hands and a
pure heart, an undivided soul that clings to You,
and a tongue that is under Your control.
Grant that Your blessing would be upon me,
and make me diligent in today's endeavors.
Amen.

For This Reason

DAY 12

Record one key reference each from your readings in Numbers, Psalms, and Proverbs:

Turn your references into a prayer.

DAY 13

Scripture: Deuteronomy 1–12; Psalms 25 and 26; Proverbs 13

Behold, I have set the land before you: go in and possess the land which the Lord sware unto your fathers, Abraham, Isaac, and Jacob, to give unto them and to their seed after them.

Deuteronomy 1:8

My foot standeth in an even place: in the congregations will I bless the Lord.

Psalm 26:12

Hope deferred maketh the heart sick: but when the desire cometh, it is a tree of life.

Proverbs 13:12

*Giving Father,
there is little that brings joy to my heart
like the fulfillment of one of Your promises in my life.
Just as You caused Your people Israel to inherit
a pleasant land, so cause me to inherit a special portion
of "land" on this fading parcel called Earth.
Let my foot stand in an even place.
Let me bless Your good and perfect name.
Thank You for the fulfillment of desire;
it truly is a tree of life and refreshment.
Amen.*

For This Reason

DAY 13

Record one key reference each from your readings in Deuteronomy, Psalms, and Proverbs:

Turn your references into a prayer.

DAY 14

Scripture: Deuteronomy 13–23; Psalms 27 and 28; Proverbs 14

Ye shall walk after the LORD your God, and fear Him, and keep His commandments, and obey His voice, and ye shall serve Him, and cleave unto Him.

Deuteronomy 13:4

When Thou saidst, Seek ye My face; my heart said unto Thee, Thy face, LORD, will I seek.

Psalm 27:8

He that walketh in his uprightness feareth the LORD: but he that is perverse in his ways despiseth Him.

Proverbs 14:2

*Tender Father,
I long to walk after You, fear You, and
keep Your word. I long to be obedient
in my service to You and cleave to You wholeheartedly.
Turn areas of half-hearted devotion
into full-fledged allegiance to You.
Increase my love for Your Word and
for Your name. I seek Your face, Lord.
Cause me to walk uprightly and give me a spirit of zeal.
Reveal any perverseness and wrongdoing
in my heart, and lead me in the way everlasting.
Amen.*

For This Reason

DAY 14

Record one key reference each from your readings in Deuteronomy, Psalms, and Proverbs:

Turn your references into a prayer.

For This Reason

DAY 15

Scripture: Deuteronomy 24–34; Psalms 29 and 30; Proverbs 15

There is none like unto the God of Jeshurun, who rideth upon the heaven in thy help, and in His excellency on the sky.

Deuteronomy 33:26

I will extol thee, O Lord; for Thou hast lifted me up, and hast not made my foes to rejoice over me.

Psalm 30:1

The way of life is above to the wise.

Proverbs 15:24

*Exalted Father,
there is none like You and none but You.
You ride over the heavens and are exalted
over all the earth. Your name and Your power are
glorious and incomparable! I extol You, O Lord,
for You lift me up and allow me to triumph
over my enemies, and You give me cause to rejoice.
I praise You for Your infinite wisdom.
Your virtues are too many to recount.
Help me today to fix my eyes on things above,
where You are seated, exalted, and enthroned.
Amen.*

For This Reason

DAY 15

Record one key reference each from your readings in Deuteronomy, Psalms, and Proverbs:

Turn your references into a prayer.

DAY 16

Scripture: Galatians 1–6; Psalms 31 and 32; Proverbs 16

But as then he that was born after the flesh persecuted him that was born after the Spirit, even so it is now.

Galatians 4:29

Thou shalt hide them in the secret of Thy presence from the pride of man: Thou shalt keep them secretly in a pavilion from the strife of tongues. Blessed be the LORD: for He hath shewed me His marvellous kindness in a strong city.

Psalm 31:20–21

The lot is cast into the lap; but the whole disposing thereof is of the LORD.

Proverbs 16:33

*Father,
from the beginning of time You have
separated and placed Your distinguishing mark
upon those born of Your Spirit. I praise You that
I am one of Your chosen and appointed for a
certain suffering and persecution.
Hide me in the secret of Your holy pavilion.
Show me Your marvelous kindness.
Lead me to Your strong and abiding city.
The lot of my life is cast by You, and I am safe in You.
Amen.*

For This Reason

DAY 16

Record one key reference each from your readings
in Galatians, Psalms, and Proverbs:

Turn your references into a prayer.

DAY 17

Scripture: Joshua 1–12; Psalms 33 and 34; Proverbs 17

And the sun stood still, and the moon stayed, until the people had avenged themselves upon their enemies. Is not this written in the book of Jasher? So the sun stood still in the midst of heaven, and hasted not to go down about a whole day.
Joshua 10:13

For He spake, and it was done; He commanded, and it stood fast.
Psalm 33:9

He that hath knowledge spareth his words: and a man of understanding is of an excellent spirit.
Proverbs 17:27

Great Creator God,
You made the sun and moon to stand still for
Your servant Joshua by just Your word.
You spoke, and it was done.
You commanded, and it stood fast.
Help me to remember that it is Your word
that holds power and that my words should be few.
As you gave Your servant Joshua both understanding and
an excellent spirit, so give me the same.
Amen.

For This Reason

DAY 17

Record one key reference each from your readings in Joshua, Psalms, and Proverbs:

Turn your references into a prayer.

For This Reason

DAY 18

Scripture: Joshua 13–24; Psalms 35 and 36; Proverbs 18

And I have given you a land for which ye did not labour, and cities which ye built not, and ye dwell in them; of the vineyards and oliveyards which ye planted not do ye eat.

Joshua 24:13

They shall be abundantly satisfied with the fatness of thy house; and thou shalt make them drink of the river of thy pleasures.

Psalm 36:8

The name of the Lord is a strong tower: the righteous runneth into it, and is safe.

Proverbs 18:10

*Benevolent Father,
each physical blessing I enjoy on earth is an
undeserved gift from You. You have placed me
in a land of abundance and have given me much
to freely enjoy. Father, forgive me for taking
such daily realities for granted.
Make my spirit abundantly satisfied with
Your presence and Your Word today.
Preserve me in Your name.
Amen.*

For This Reason

DAY 18

Record one key reference each from your readings in Joshua, Psalms, and Proverbs:

Turn your references into a prayer.

DAY 19

Scripture: *Judges 1–12; Psalms 37 and 38; Proverbs 19*

Then Jael Heber's wife took a nail of the tent, and took an hammer in her hand, and went softly unto him, and smote the nail into his temples, and fastened it into the ground: for he was fast asleep and weary. So he died.

Judges 4:21

And he shall bring forth thy righteousness as the light, and thy judgment as the noonday.

Psalm 37:6

The fear of the LORD tendeth to life: and he that hath it shall abide satisfied; he shall not be visited with evil.

Proverbs 19:23

*Righteous Father,
make me as fearless and bold as Jael
toward all that is evil. Help me to be aggressive in my
stance toward evil, and show me how to deal with
areas that hinder my walk with You. Grant me a
spirit of wisdom and discernment and the ability to
bring a "hammer" down on anything that is not of You.
Bring forth my righteousness, and judge me
according to Your great mercy. Let me abide and be
satisfied in knowing You.
Amen.*

For This Reason

DAY 19

Record one key reference each from your readings in Judges, Psalms, and Proverbs:

Turn your references into a prayer.

For This Reason

DAY 20

Scripture: Judges 13–21; Psalms 39 and 40; Proverbs 20

In those days there was no king in Israel: every man did that which was right in his own eyes.

Judges 21:25

LORD, make me to know mine end, and the measure of my days, what it is: that I may know how frail I am.

Psalm 39:4

Man's goings are of the LORD; how can a man then understand his own way?

Proverbs 20:24

*Wise Father,
how foolish I am when I enter into my day
without Your Word in my heart and on my tongue.
How often my life sounds like a chapter out of Israel's
history, and I simply do what is right
in my own eyes. Gracious Father, forgive me.
Make me to know my end and the measure
of my days. Cause me to glimpse my own frailty, and
contrast it continually with Your great and
unchanging majesty. Show me the way I should go,
and give me an understanding and discerning heart.
Amen.*

For This Reason

DAY 20

Record one key reference each from your readings in Judges, Psalms, and Proverbs:

Turn your references into a prayer.

For This Reason

DAY 21

Scripture: Ruth 1–4; Psalms 41 and 42; Proverbs 21

The LORD recompense thy work, and a full reward be given thee of the LORD God of Israel, under whose wings thou art come to trust.
Ruth 2:12

And as for me, Thou upholdest me in mine integrity, and settest me before Thy face for ever.
Psalm 41:12

He that followeth after righteousness and mercy findeth life, righteousness, and honour.
Proverbs 21:21

*Loving Father,
cause me to work wholeheartedly for You
without seeking the promotion, attention, or favor
of others. Like Ruth, let me be fully given to
the task that you have set before me.
Let me be a servant to others.
Like Ruth, place me under the wing of Your care.
Uphold me and help me to walk the straight line of
integrity, following after mercy and righteousness.
Favor me, Father, with Your love and honor.
Amen.*

For This Reason

DAY 21

Record one key reference each from your readings in Ruth, Psalms, and Proverbs:

Turn your references into a prayer.

For This Reason

DAY 22

Scripture: 1 Samuel 1-15; Psalms 43 and 44; Proverbs 22

Moreover as for me, God forbid that I should sin against the LORD in ceasing to pray for you: but I will teach you the good and the right way.

1 Samuel 12:23

If we have forgotten the name of our God, or stretched out our hands to a strange god; Shall not God search this out? for He knoweth the secrets of the heart.

Psalm 44:20-21

Seest thou a man diligent in his business? he shall stand before kings; he shall not stand before mean men.

Proverbs 22:29

Faithful Father,
Your servant Samuel compels me to see
that when I cease to pray for others,
I sin against You. Keep me in an attitude of prayer today,
and all the more toward those who are difficult to love.
Let me not forget the power in and of Your name.
You alone are familiar with my inmost thoughts,
and You know the secrets of my heart.
Keep me diligent in Your way, and
let me stand before kings.
Amen.

For This Reason

DAY 22

Record one key reference each from your readings in 1 Samuel, Psalms, and Proverbs:

Turn your references into a prayer.

DAY 23

Scripture: 1 Samuel 16–31; Psalms 45 and 46; Proverbs 23

And Jonathan stripped himself of the robe that was upon him, and gave it to David, and his garments, even to his sword, and to his bow, and to his girdle.

1 Samuel 18:4

Thou lovest righteousness, and hatest wickedness: therefore God, Thy God, hath anointed Thee with the oil of gladness above Thy fellows.

Psalm 45:7

Apply thine heart unto instruction, and thine ears to the words of knowledge.

Proverbs 23:12

*Gentle Father,
how drawn I am by Jonathan's example
of humility and complete trust in You.
As successor to the throne, he could have held tightly
to his earthly rights and his kingly position.
He didn't. He gave up the lesser for the greater and
was simply obedient to You. Let me apply my heart to
Jonathan's example. Grant me a spirit of true
humility today, Lord.
Amen.*

For This Reason

DAY 23

Record one key reference each from your readings in 1 Samuel, Psalms, and Proverbs:

Turn your references into a prayer.

DAY 24

Scripture: 2 Samuel 1–12; Psalms 47 and 48; Proverbs 24

So David and all the house of Israel brought up the ark of the LORD with shouting, and with the sound of the trumpet.

2 Samuel 6:15

Sing praises to God, sing praises: sing praises unto our King, sing praises. For God is the King of all the earth: sing ye praises with understanding.

Psalm 47: 6–7

Every man shall kiss his lips that giveth a right answer.

Proverbs 24:26

Glorious Father,
corporate worship, such as Israel shared with
King David, was grand and glorious.
The recognition that Your presence was in their midst
was worth celebrating. It still is! The fruit of lips giving
praise to Your name is excellent and acknowledged by You.
The Psalmist says "sing" four times.
Let our lips move in one accord, giving You
the praise that is due Your name.
Let corporate rejoicing resound!
Amen.

For This Reason

DAY 24

Record one key reference each from your readings in 2 Samuel, Psalms, and Proverbs:

Turn your references into a prayer.

DAY 25

Scripture: 2 Samuel 13–24; Psalms 49 and 50; Proverbs 25

And David went up by the ascent of mount Olivet, and wept as he went up, and had his head covered, and he went barefoot: and all the people that was with him covered every man his head, and they went up, weeping as they went up.

2 Samuel 15:30

Wherefore should I fear in the days of evil, when the iniquity of my heels shall compass me about?

Psalm 49:5

As he that taketh away a garment in cold weather, and as vinegar upon nitre, so is he that singeth songs to an heavy heart.

Proverbs 25:20

Forgiving Father,
You are familiar and acquainted with my grief,
identifying with my despair even when I, like David,
am facing the consequences of my own sin.
The same mount David ascended, You ascended for me.
Thank you for rescuing me from the dominion of sin and darkness, and for applying the remedy of grace to a heavy heart. Compass me with Your love and mercy.
Amen.

For This Reason

DAY 25

Record one key reference each from your readings in 2 Samuel, Psalms, and Proverbs:

Turn your references into a prayer.

DAY 26

Scripture: Ephesians 1–6; Psalms 51 and 52; Proverbs 26

Let no corrupt communication proceed out of your mouth, but that which is good to the use of edifying, that it may minister grace unto the hearers.

Ephesians 4:29

O Lord, open Thou my lips; and my mouth shall shew forth Thy praise.
Psalm 51:15

Where no wood is, there the fire goeth out: so where there is no talebearer, the strife ceaseth.
Proverbs 26:20

Gracious Father,
I am responsible today for the words I speak and the thoughts and ideas that I voice to another.
Would You put a muzzle on my tongue, Lord, and a check in my spirit when I offend You or hurt another today? Would You teach me how to turn gossip into grace and slander into sympathy?
Let my mouth be an instrument of encouragement, and let my lips show forth Your praise. Cast away compromising verbal kindling and use my tongue for healing today. Amen.

For This Reason

DAY 26

Record one key reference each from your readings in Ephesians, Psalms, and Proverbs:

Turn your references into a prayer.

For This Reason

DAY 27

***Scripture: 1 Kings 1–11; Psalms 53 and 54;
Proverbs 27***

For it came to pass, when Solomon was old, that his wives turned away his heart after other gods: and his heart was not perfect with the Lord his God, as was the heart of David his father.
1 Kings 11:4

Every one of them is gone back: they are altogether become filthy; there is none that doeth good, no, not one.
Psalm 53:3

Hell and destruction are never full; so the eyes of man are never satisfied.
Proverbs 27:20

❧

*Pure and Holy Father,
You blessed Solomon with a supernatural wisdom,
and yet even that could not save him from the desire and
passion of his flesh. We choose poorly and act badly
when the object of our affection is not You, Lord.
Give me the favor of your servant David.
Thank You that You are rich in
forgiveness and mercy when I sin.
Keep my eye satisfied with Your glory.
Amen.*

For This Reason

DAY 27

Record one key reference each from your readings in 1 Kings, Psalms, and Proverbs:

Turn your references into a prayer.

For This Reason

DAY 28

Scripture: 1 Kings 12–22; Psalms 55 and 56; Proverbs 28

And the ravens brought him bread and flesh in the morning, and bread and flesh in the evening; and he drank of the brook.
1 Kings 17:6

Cast thy burden upon the Lord, and He shall sustain thee: He shall never suffer the righteous to be moved.
Psalm 55:22

Whoso walketh uprightly shall be saved: but he that is perverse in his ways shall fall at once.
Proverbs 28:18

*Sustaining Father,
ravens were an unclean animal, and yet
You chose them to be the divine carriers of
Your provision. Thank You for the unexpected ravens You
select for my life and for the provision You grant me
through them. I cast my every care upon You today, Lord,
assured that in Your time and in Your way, You will meet
each need in my life and sustain me. Feed me from
Your word and keep me upright; do not allow
my foot to slip. Be my sure supply, and
keep me in step with You. Amen.*

For This Reason

DAY 28

Record one key reference each from your readings in 1 Kings, Psalms, and Proverbs:

Turn your references into a prayer.

For This Reason

DAY 29

Scripture: 2 Kings 1–12; Psalms 57 and 58; Proverbs 29

Then went he down, and dipped himself seven times in Jordan, according to the saying of the man of God: and his flesh came again like unto the flesh of a little child, and he was clean.
2 Kings 5:14

For Thy mercy is great unto the heavens, and Thy truth unto the clouds.
Psalm 57:10

A man's pride shall bring him low: but honour shall uphold the humble in spirit.
Proverbs 29:23

*Powerful Father,
how You long for me to experience the
greatness, majesty, and might of Your power, and how
often You find me questioning You, as Naaman did.
Father, be merciful to me, and forgive my unbelief.
Do not let me forego seeing Your hand at work today
because of an unclean and unbelieving heart.
Cleanse my spirit, mind, and body.
Send Your truth into my soul, and
grant me a spirit of humility.
Amen.*

For This Reason

DAY 29

Record one key reference each from your readings in 2 Kings, Psalms, and Proverbs:

Turn your references into a prayer.

DAY 30

Scripture: 2 Kings 13–25; Psalms 59 and 60; Proverbs 30

And the remnant that is escaped of the house of Judah shall yet again take root downward, and bear fruit upward.

2 Kings 19:30

Unto Thee, O my strength, will I sing: for God is my defence, and the God of my mercy.

Psalm 59:17

Every word of God is pure: He is a shield unto them that put their trust in Him.

Proverbs 30:5

*Enduring Father,
time and time again You forgive me
and remind me that, what You did for Israel,
You also do for me. Preserving me from utter ruin,
You lovingly cause me to take root downward
and bear fruit upward when I call out to You
and rely on You. You are my strength, a pillar to me.
You are my defense and my glory, and I give You praise.
Your Word is a shield to me,
and I willingly put my trust in You.
Amen.*

For This Reason

DAY 30

Record one key reference each from your readings in 2 Kings, Psalms, and Proverbs:

Turn your references into a prayer.

For This Reason

DAY 31

Scripture: Philippians 1–4; Psalms 61 and 62; Proverbs 31

Being confident of this very thing, that He which hath begun a good work in you will perform it until the day of Jesus Christ.
Philippians 1:6

From the end of the earth will I cry unto Thee, when my heart is overwhelmed: lead me to the rock that is higher than I.
Psalm 61:2

Open thy mouth, judge righteously, and plead the cause of the poor and needy.
Proverbs 31:9

*Father, my perfector,
everything on earth is susceptible to change but You.
You are the same, and Your years have no end.
What confidence I ought to have: From the beginning
to the end of my life, Your presence will abide with me and
perform through me the works ordained for me.
When I am fearful, establish me on that immovable Rock.
Your ways are infinitely good and worthy of my praise.
And as You have been faithful to look upon my poor and
needy state, let me be responsive to others
in the same condition. Amen.*

For This Reason

DAY 31

Record one key reference each from your readings in Philippians, Psalms, and Proverbs:

Turn your references into a prayer.

For This Reason

DAY 32

Scripture: 1 Chronicles 1–15; Psalms 63 and 64

And these are the singers, chief of the fathers of the Levites, who remaining in the chambers were free: for they were employed in that work day and night.

1 Chronicles 9:33

Because Thy lovingkindness is better than life, my lips shall praise Thee.

Psalm 63:3

*Worthy Father,
worship, expressed through music and song,
was designed by You for Your glory
in Your holy dwelling from long ago.
Day and night, song was put forth;
the sacrifice of praise was poured out to You,
because Your lovingkindness is better than life.
What a precious thing You instituted for
Your dwelling place among men!
Employ my mouth for Your praise today,
so that another is drawn into a
holy place of worship to You.
Amen.*

For This Reason

DAY 32

Record one key reference each from your readings in 1 Chronicles and Psalms:

Turn your references into a prayer.

DAY 33

Scripture: 1 Chronicles 16–29; Psalms 65 and 66

But who am I, and what is my people, that we should be able to offer so willingly after this sort? for all things come of Thee, and of Thine own have we given Thee. For we are strangers before Thee, and sojourners, as were all our fathers: our days on the earth are as a shadow, and there is none abiding.

1 Chronicles 29:14–15

Blessed is the man whom Thou choosest, and causest to approach unto Thee, that he may dwell in Thy courts: we shall be satisfied with the goodness of Thy house, even of thy holy temple.

Psalm 65:4

Excellent Father,
I am moved to my knees in wonder, as David was,
by Your wondrous hand and tangible grace upon my life.
Truly Your mercy cannot be described in words.
You grant me an undeserved, eternal rank and appoint me
a desirable earthly station; You delight in revealing
Yourself to me. You give to me immeasurably more than
I need, and anything I give back to You
is merely a token of Your grace.
I am chosen, beloved, and sealed for Your courts.
I am blessed.
Amen.

For This Reason

DAY 33

Record one key reference each from your readings in 1 Chronicles and Psalms:

Turn your references into a prayer.

DAY 34

Scripture: 2 Chronicles 1–12; Psalms 67 and 68

Notwithstanding thou shalt not build the house; but thy son which shall come forth out of thy loins, he shall build the house for My name.

2 Chronicles 6:9

Blessed be the Lord, who daily loadeth us with benefits, even the God of our salvation. Selah.

Psalm 68:19

*Ordaining Father,
Your servant David had it in his heart
to build You a temple, but You had already ordained
that work for his son Solomon. This encourages me,
for in like manner You have laid Your hand upon me and
established a work for me to do, and it will not be
given to another. It is this knowledge and grace
that fills my life with purpose.
Thank you for the countless personal benefits
You extend to me, Lord.
You are the God of my deliverance
and the God of a thousand mercies;
surely You are worthy of my praise.
Amen.*

For This Reason

DAY 34

Record one key reference each from your readings in 2 Chronicles and Psalms:

Turn your references into a prayer.

For This Reason

DAY 35

Scripture: 2 Chronicles 13–25; Psalms 69 and 70

And Asa cried unto the LORD his God, and said, LORD, it is nothing with Thee to help, whether with many, or with them that have no power: help us, O LORD our God; for we rest on Thee, and in Thy name we go against this multitude. O LORD, Thou art our God; let no man prevail against Thee.
2 Chronicles 14:11

But I am poor and needy: make haste unto me, O God: Thou art my help and my deliverer; O LORD, make no tarrying.
Psalm 70:5

*Empowering Father,
I come to You in all my weakness
and desperation, as Asa did, and cast myself
on Your mercy. You are not looking for any strength
that I possess, or any power that I might wield.
You are seeking eyes that look to You,
and confidence in Your power and Your name.
You are looking for me to trust You.
So I approach You today, Lord, in a
desperate, poor, and needy state,
thankful that You will empower me. Amen.*

For This Reason

DAY 35

Record one key reference each from your readings in 2 Chronicles and Psalms:

Turn your references into a prayer.

For This Reason

DAY 36

Scripture: 2 Chronicles 26–36; Psalms 71 and 72

And Hezekiah rejoiced, and all the people, that God had prepared the people: for the thing was done suddenly.

2 Chronicles 29:36

Blessed be the Lord God, the God of Israel, who only doeth wondrous things. And blessed be His glorious name for ever: and let the whole earth be filled with His glory; Amen, and Amen.

Psalm 72:18–19

Exacting Father,
You placed it on Hezekiah's heart to reinstitute
the feast of Passover and to kindle remembrance
of Your faithfulness. Hezekiah's immediate and obedient
response to You ushered in a powerful glimpse
of Your glory. Not only did you allow Hezekiah to achieve
and fulfill Your desires, but You did the thing suddenly:
You orchestrated a timeline that was of Your doing,
so that not even King Hezekiah could glory
in a personal achievement.
Great God who does wondrous things,
perform a sudden work in my life
that attests to Your glory.
I will rejoice in what You do. Amen.

For This Reason

DAY 36

Record one key reference each from your readings in 2 Chronicles and Psalms:

Turn your references into a prayer.

DAY 37

Scripture: Colossians 1–4; Psalms 73 and 74

For by Him were all things created, that are in heaven, and that are in earth, visible and invisible, whether they be thrones, or dominions, or principalities, or powers: all things were created by Him, and for Him: And He is before all things, and by Him all things consist.

Colossians 1:16–17

For God is my King of old, working salvation in the midst of the earth.

Psalm 74:12

*Exalted Father,
from atoms to individuals, from
elements to forces, Lord, You created them all.
Your sovereign hand governs each aspect
of creation with divine precision.
This reality should cause me to see that
nothing can happen in my life without
Your hand orchestrating its specific purpose.
Forgive me for my constant fretting
and for the way I forget Your power.
You are my God and my King, and the praise
and provider of my life. Work in my midst
as You did in days of old,
and let me be quick to recount
Your faithfulness in my life. Amen.*

For This Reason

DAY 37

Record one key reference each from your readings in Colossians and Psalms:

Turn your references into a prayer.

For This Reason

DAY 38

Scripture: Ezra 1–10; Psalms 75 and 76

For Ezra had prepared his heart to seek the law of the Lord, and to do it, and to teach in Israel statutes and judgments.
Ezra 7:10

All the horns of the wicked also will I cut off; but the horns of the righteous shall be exalted.
Psalm 75:10

☙

Observant Father,
Your eyes range throughout the whole earth.
Those who zealously followed You
were observed and known by You.
Like Ezra, I long to have a prepared heart
for seeking after You. Like Ezra, I want to do
Your Word before I teach Your Word.
I long to be commended as a faithful servant
of Yours, Lord, and to be found in constant union
and communion with You. Thank You for the
divine power that separates and drives apart
the wicked from the righteous.
Exalt the horn of the upright, and let
all those who fear and love Your name
inherit favor from on high. Amen.

For This Reason

DAY 38

Record one key reference each from your readings in Ezra and Psalms:

Turn your references into a prayer.

For This Reason

DAY 39

Scripture: Nehemiah 1–13; Psalms 77 and 78

Remember me, O my God, concerning this, and wipe not out my good deeds that I have done for the house of my God, and for the offices thereof.

Nehemiah 13:14

They kept not the covenant of God, and refused to walk in His law; and forgat His works, and His wonders that He had shewed them.
Psalm 78:10–11

༄

*Rewarding Father,
it's so easy to grow lazy and lethargic in Your work,
and to succumb to an attitude of laxness.
Father, wake my spirit! Let me labor heartily for You,
as Your servant Nehemiah did, trusting that You will
recompense each work I complete for Your name.
Cause me to hunger for Your Word, to meditate
on Your Word continually, and to recount Your Word
faithfully. Remember me, O my God,
and the labor performed for You.
Let me not forget Your faithfulness.
Forgive my doubt and unbelief, and the times
I fail to to speak of You or walk intentionally with You.
Help me to remember Your ways.
Amen.*

For This Reason

DAY 39

Record one key reference each from your readings in Nehemiah and Psalms:

Turn your references into a prayer.

For This Reason

DAY 40

Scripture: Esther 1–10; Psalms 79 and 80

Now when the turn of Esther, the daughter of Abihail the uncle of Mordecai, who had taken her for his daughter, was come to go in unto the king, she required nothing but what Hegai the king's chamberlain, the keeper of the women, appointed. And Esther obtained favour in the sight of all them that looked upon her.

Esther 2:15

Return, we beseech thee, O God of hosts: look down from heaven, and behold, and visit this vine.

Psalm 80:14

Father, our provider,
Esther was a beautiful and chosen
young vine of Yours. She exemplified qualities that
far exceeded her external beauty.
Trusting You for her provision,
she lacked nothing and she wanted nothing,
but only what she was given.
In Esther's life I am challenged to a deeper level of
contentment. I am challenged, Lord, to look to You more
often and to thank You more frequently for the favor
You show to me continually.
Look down from heaven and visit this vine.
Amen.

For This Reason

DAY 40

Record one key reference each from your readings in Esther and Psalms:

Turn your references into a prayer.

For This Reason

DAY 41

Scripture: Job 1–14; Psalms 81 and 82

Though He slay me, yet will I trust in Him: but I will maintain mine own ways before Him. He also shall be my salvation: for an hypocrite shall not come before Him.

Job 13:15–16

Arise, O God, judge the earth: for Thou shalt inherit all nations.

Psalm 82:8

❦

Intimate Father,
to hold fast to You during calamitous times is
a powerful testimony of Your work in me.
Unlike Job, I have the constant and precious
presence of the Holy Spirit, who leads me,
guides me, and interprets Your Word to me through
the afflictions and difficulties I face. You have not left
me alone; You will never leave me nor forsake me.
Father, You are the righteous King and Judge,
not only of all nations, but of my heart.
Inhabit my spirit, and help me to maintain an
attitude of trust in You in my present difficulty.
Amen.

For This Reason

DAY 41

Record one key reference each from your readings in Job and Psalms:

Turn your references into a prayer.

DAY 42

Scripture: Job 15–28; Psalms 83 and 84

But He knoweth the way that I take: when He hath tried me, I shall come forth as gold. My foot hath held His steps, His way have I kept, and not declined. Neither have I gone back from the commandment of His lips; I have esteemed the words of His mouth more than my necessary food… For He performeth the thing that is appointed for me: and many such things are with Him.

Job 23:10–12, 14

O Lord of hosts, blessed is the man that trusteth in Thee.

Psalm 84:12

*Trustworthy Father,
You know the way that I take and the trials
You have selected for my life. I can praise You in them
because they are controlled by Your sovereign hand
and purposed for my growth and my good.
No matter what my emotions, I shall come forth
as gold as I am obedient to You, for You shall
preserve my way. Your presence and Your Word
are never absent from me, and You will
perform the thing appointed for me.
O Lord of hosts, I am blessed in You,
and I trust You to appoint a path
that will lead me closer to You.
Amen.*

For This Reason

DAY 42

Record one key reference each from your readings in Job and Psalms:

Turn your references into a prayer.

DAY 43

Scripture: Job 29–42; Psalms 85 and 86

And the Lord turned the captivity of Job, when he prayed for his friends: also the Lord gave Job twice as much as he had before…So the Lord blessed the latter end of Job more than his beginning.

Job 42:10, 12a

Shew me a token for good; that they which hate me may see it, and be ashamed: because Thou, Lord, hast holpen me, and comforted me.

Psalm 86:17

*Restoring Father,
all Your ways are right, pure and good,
even when I don't understand them.
As You did for Your servant Job, turn a
present arena of captivity in my life
into a platform that reveals Your power and glory.
Bless my latter days on earth with double,
and grant spiritual provision that exceeds
my early days; restore the years the
locusts have eaten. Show me a token of good,
and comfort me in the presence
of my enemies.
Amen.*

For This Reason

DAY 43

Record one key reference each from your readings in Job and Psalms:

Turn your references into a prayer.

DAY 44

Scripture: Ecclesiastes 1–12; Psalms 87 and 88

I know that, whatsoever God doeth, it shall be for ever: nothing can be put to it, nor any thing taken from it: and God doeth it, that men should fear before Him.

Ecclesiastes 3:14

All my springs are in thee.

Psalm 87:7b

Omnipotent Father,
You are Alpha and Omega, the beginning
and the end. There is none like You!
All things are sovereignly assigned
by Your hand. You create a timeline and
map out my destiny; You perform the thing
appointed for me. Nothing can be added to it,
and nothing removed from it.
The people, events, and trials that enter my life,
however difficult or evil they may seem,
cannot exist apart from Your foreordained knowledge
and plan. What a marvelous reality this is to me, Lord.
No human, force, or power can diminish Your Word.
Once You have spoken, Your Word is settled;
forever it shall stand.
All my springs are in You.
Amen.

For This Reason

DAY 44

Record one key reference each from your readings in Ecclesiastes and Psalms:

Turn your references into a prayer.

For This Reason

DAY 45

Scripture: Song of Solomon 1–8; Psalms 89 and 90

I am my beloved's, and his desire is toward me.
Song of Solomon 7:10

Blessed is the people that know the joyful sound: they shall walk, O Lord, in the light of Thy countenance. In Thy name shall they rejoice all the day: and in Thy righteousness shall they be exalted.
Psalm 89:15–16

My Father,
what a wonder to be Your child,
Your beloved one. I rejoice today in the knowledge that
I am in a love relationship with You, pursued by You,
and chosen by You. My life and conduct here on earth
are my response to Your love; oh, that they might be used
for Your glory and the exaltation of Your glorious Name!
Shine the light of Your countenance inside my heart,
and lead me into a spirit of song and rejoicing.
Your name and Your righteousness are my glory;
let them lead me to Your holy hill.
Elevate me in Your righteousness, align me in Your truth,
and position me on earth to live
in the realm of Your glory.
Amen.

For This Reason

DAY 45

Record one key reference each from your readings
in the Song of Solomon and Psalms:

Turn your references into a prayer.

DAY 46

Scripture: Isaiah 1–14; Psalms 91 and 92

Say ye to the righteous, that it shall be well with him: for they shall eat the fruit of their doings. Woe unto the wicked! it shall be ill with him: for the reward of his hands shall be given him.

Isaiah 3:10–11

The righteous shall flourish like the palm tree: he shall grow like a cedar in Lebanon. Those that be planted in the house of the Lord shall flourish in the courts of our God.

Psalm 92:12–13

Blessed Father,
"It shall be well with him."
These words will be linked to the person abiding
in Christ. Blessing will not be removed from this soul.
"It shall be ill with him."
These words will be uttered to the person
who has rejected Christ and chosen his own way.
Lord, impart a concern in my heart for the lost
and those destined for destruction.
Help me to consider their end. I give You praise that
I am made righteous in Christ and that one day
I will flourish and dwell in Your courts.
Amen.

For This Reason

DAY 46

Record one key reference each from your readings in Isaiah and Psalms:

Turn your references into a prayer.

For This Reason

DAY 47

Scripture: Isaiah 15-26; Psalms 93 and 94

Thou wilt keep him in perfect peace, whose mind is stayed on Thee: because he trusteth in Thee. Trust ye in the Lord for ever: for in the Lord Jehovah is everlasting strength.

Isaiah 26:3-4

The Lord reigneth, He is clothed with majesty; the Lord is clothed with strength, wherewith He hath girded Himself: the world also is stablished, that it cannot be moved. Thy throne is established of old: Thou art from everlasting.

Psalm 93:1-2

*Unchanging Father,
there is no variance in Your character or word,
so the longer my mind is stayed on You,
the greater tranquillity I will experience.
A life of peace is simply a life lived in living trust of You.
You reign over all and are sovereignly orchestrating
all things on earth for Your glory and purpose.
You are clothed with majesty and strength,
and girded with might and power.
The world hinges its very existence on Your Word.
You are JEHOVAH!
Perfect peace is mine in You.
Amen.*

For This Reason

DAY 47

Record one key reference each from your readings in Isaiah and Psalms:

Turn your references into a prayer.

For This Reason

DAY 48

Scripture: Isaiah 27–40; Psalms 95 and 96

And though the Lord give you the bread of adversity, and the water of affliction, yet shall not thy Teachers be removed into a corner any more, but thine eyes shall see thy Teachers: And thine ears shall hear a word behind thee, saying, This is the way, walk ye in it, when ye turn to the right hand, and when ye turn to the left.

Isaiah 30:20–21

Harden not your heart, as in the provocation, and as in the day of temptation in the wilderness.

Psalm 95:8

~

Faithful Father,
if I did not believe that adversity and affliction
filtered through Your sovereign hand, how dreadful
would be this present trial and crisis. Instead, I confidently
trust that in this difficult place I shall be given wisdom,
instruction, and discernment. You will not leave me to
make decisions on my own. You will induce responses
from Your Spirit while I am feeding on Your Word
to direct my every step. The bread and water of adversity
will produce growth, and You will conform me to
Your Son through them. Let me not deviate from Your
Word or provoke Your Spirit. Amen.

For This Reason

DAY 48

Record one key reference each from your readings in Isaiah and Psalms:

Turn your references into a prayer.

For This Reason

DAY 49

Scripture: Isaiah 40–53; Psalms 97 and 98

Fear thou not; for I am with thee: be not dismayed; for I am thy God: I will strengthen thee; yea, I will help thee; yea, I will uphold thee with the right hand of My righteousness.
Isaiah 41:10

O sing unto the Lord a new song; for He hath done marvellous things: His right hand, and His holy arm, hath gotten Him the victory.
Psalm 98:1

*Victorious Father,
my greatest fear and most oppressive trial
cannot come close to matching the majesty
and might of Your sufficient right hand.
You will prevail, not in most situations, but in all.
For this reason I can rejoice.
I can be sure that, regardless of what this day holds,
You will accomplish a spiritual victory through my life.
You delight in performing the impossible
through me, and You withhold no good thing
from me. You will supply strength in my weakness,
hope in my helplessness,
and victory in my trial.
Amen.*

For This Reason

DAY 49

Record one key reference each from your readings in Isaiah and Psalms:

Turn your references into a prayer.

For This Reason

DAY 50

Scripture: Isaiah 54–66; Psalms 99 and 100

For thy Maker is thine husband; the LORD of hosts is His name; and thy Redeemer the Holy One of Israel; The God of the whole earth shall He be called.

Isaiah 54:5

Know ye that the LORD He is God: it is He that hath made us, and not we ourselves; we are His people, and the sheep of His pasture.

Psalm 100:3

༄

*Comforting Father,
Your word is filled with a thousand proofs
that You love me and have made me for You:
When I forget who I am,
You remind me that You are my Maker.
When I crave intimacy, You beckon to me as husband.
When I forget who is responsible for victory,
You remind me that You are Lord of Hosts.
When I need cleansing, You remind me that You are holy.
When I am lost, You remind me that
You are my Shepherd. Thank You for the comforts that
You extend to me through Your Word
and for the intimate expressions of love
that You've given me today.
Amen.*

For This Reason

DAY 50

Record one key reference each from your readings in Isaiah and Psalms:

Turn your references into a prayer.

For This Reason

DAY 51

Scripture: Matthew 1–14; Psalms 101 and 102

Again, the kingdom of heaven is like unto treasure hid in a field; the which when a man hath found, he hideth, and for joy thereof goeth and selleth all that he hath, and buyeth that field.
Matthew 13:44

Mine eyes shall be upon the faithful of the land, that they may dwell with me: he that walketh in a perfect way, he shall serve me.
Psalm 101:6

*Priceless Father,
David believed that sacrifice to You
must always cost him something.*
He had found precious treasure through seeking You.
Father, Your Word and Your presence
are priceless treasures to me. Let me go forth with joy
and give my all for the One who has sacrificed
all for me. Let my companions be of one purpose
and one mind, and let our bond be the
hidden treasure that is worthy of all pursuit.
Amen.*

*1 Chronicles 21:24

For This Reason

DAY 51

Record one key reference each from your readings in Matthew and Psalms:

Turn your references into a prayer.

For This Reason

DAY 52

Scripture: Matthew 15–28; Psalms 103 and 104

Watch therefore, for ye know neither the day nor the hour wherein the Son of man cometh.

Matthew 25:13

As for man, his days are as grass: as a flower of the field, so he flourisheth. For the wind passeth over it, and it is gone; and the place thereof shall know it no more.

Psalm 103:15–16

*Faithful Father,
the Old Testament held countless prophecies
of Your first coming, and You did not disappoint.
The New Testament holds countless prophecies
of Your return, and You will not fail us.
Give me the longing spirit and watchful eyes of
Anna and Simeon.* Wake me from fleshly slumber and
earthly lethargy. Let my existence and purpose become
charged with an urgency to experience more of You
and speak more about You. Cause me to consider the
brevity of my life on earth and the
length of eternity with You.
Earth is not my destiny, and heaven calls me home.
Amen.*

*Luke 2:25–38.

For This Reason

DAY 52

Record one key reference each from your readings in Matthew and Psalms:

Turn your references into a prayer.

For This Reason

DAY 53

Scripture: Jeremiah 1–13; Psalms 105 and 106

For thus saith the LORD to the men of Judah and Jerusalem, Break up your fallow ground, and sow not among thorns. Circumcise yourselves to the LORD, and take away the foreskins of your heart...

Jeremiah 4:3–4a

But were mingled among the heathen, and learned their works. And they served their idols: which were a snare unto them.

Psalm 106:35–36

༄

Holy Father,
my heart needs to be cultivated
continually and sown with the pure seed of Your word.
How prone I am to sowing among the thorns
and adopting the ways and ideas of the people
and environment that surround me.
Separation has always been, and will always be,
essential to being one of Your disciples.
Father, help me to cling wholly to You.
Remove the foreskin of my heart.
Show me areas of weakness, and separate me
for a pure and noble work and purpose.
Amen.

For This Reason

DAY 53

Record one key reference each from your readings in Jeremiah and Psalms:

Turn your references into a prayer.

DAY 54

Scripture: Jeremiah 14–28; Psalms 107 and 108

Thy words were found, and I did eat them; and Thy word was unto me the joy and rejoicing of mine heart: for I am called by Thy name, O LORD God of hosts.

Jeremiah 15:16

For He satisfieth the longing soul, and filleth the hungry soul with goodness.

Psalm 107:9

*Life-indwelling Father,
the world holds out so many tantalizing
and forbidden fruits—power, fame, materialism—
but in the end each leads to death.
In contrast to the world is Your Word.
It delivers me a daily portion of truth and grace
and provides me with the daily nutrients
necessary for transformation and growth.
Father, I love You, and I love Your Word!
You bring me wholeness, joy, and rejoicing.
Your name frames my entire being, and I am Yours.
Thank you for indwelling me, filling me,
and satisfying me with Your goodness.
Amen.*

For This Reason

DAY 54

Record one key reference each from your readings in Jeremiah and Psalms:

Turn your references into a prayer.

For This Reason

DAY 55

Scripture: Jeremiah 29–41; Psalms 109 and 110

So they drew up Jeremiah with cords, and took him up out of the dungeon: and Jeremiah remained in the court of the prison.
Jeremiah 38:13

I will greatly praise the LORD with my mouth; yea, I will praise Him among the multitude. For He shall stand at the right hand of the poor, to save him from those that condemn his soul.
Psalm 109:30–31

All-knowing God,
Jeremiah was a popular prophet with an unpopular message, and the proclamation of that message—repentance—landed him in a dungeon.
Like many of the saints, he was subject to temporary ill-treatment. I may experience the same:
Suffering, in some form, often accompanies obedience.
But You will remain faithful in my suffering,
and the message of the gospel will never change!
I will praise You, Lord, with my mouth, and sing about You in the multitude. You will deliver me and draw me with cords of lovingkindness.
You are at my right hand, and I shall not be moved.
Amen.

For This Reason

DAY 55

Record one key reference each from your readings in Jeremiah and Psalms:

Turn your references into a prayer.

DAY 56

Scripture: Jeremiah 42–52; Psalms 111 and 112

He hath made the earth by His power, He hath established the world by His wisdom, and hath stretched out the heaven by His understanding.

Jeremiah 51:15

The works of the LORD are great, sought out of all them that have pleasure therein. His work is honourable and glorious: and His righteousness endureth for ever.

Psalm 111:2–3

*Omnipotent Father,
power, wisdom, and understanding
belong to You, and You are the complete fulfillment
and embodiment of all three.
What a wonder!
Today I fill my list with praise to You,
thanking You for creating this world
filled with wonder—a planet teeming with life,
with heavens that canopy me.
Your works and creation are a manifestation
of Your faithfulness to man, in spite of
our unfaithfulness to You. You are worthy of praise.
Cause me to rejoice in all Your hands have made.
Amen.*

For This Reason

DAY 56

Record one key reference each from your readings in Jeremiah and Psalms:

Turn your references into a prayer.

For This Reason

DAY 57

Scripture: Lamentations 1–5; Psalms 113 and 114

It is of the LORD's mercies that we are not consumed, because His compassions fail not. They are new every morning: great is Thy faithfulness.

Lamentations 3:22–23

The LORD is high above all nations, and His glory above the heavens. Who is like unto the LORD our God, who dwelleth on high…
Psalm 113:4–5

Compassionate Father,
today I simply come to You in need of much mercy:
I am desperate.
I am weak.
I am tired.
Let Your liberal and abundant compassion
be poured out upon me. Envelop my spirit in mercy,
and saturate my mind with truth.
Thank you for a love that completely pardons
and for a grace that is given without reserve.
Your ways are infinite and high, Lord.
Your glory reaches to the heavens, and yet dwells
within man. Your compassion never fails.
Great is Your faithfulness.
Amen.

For This Reason

DAY 57

Record one key reference each from your readings in Lamentations and Psalms:

Turn your references into a prayer.

DAY 58

Scripture: Mark 1–8; Psalms 115 and 116

When Jesus heard it, He saith unto them, They that are whole have no need of the physician, but they that are sick: I came not to call the righteous, but sinners to repentance.
Mark 2:17

What shall I render unto the LORD for all His benefits toward me? I will take the cup of salvation, and call upon the name of the LORD.
Psalm 116:12–13

Great Physician,
Your eyes have always favored the poor,
the sick, the needy, and the destitute.
From lepers to paraplegics,
from castaways to prostitutes,
You walked among them and loved them—
and I was among them.
I do not have sufficient praise to give You
for all the grace You have lovingly lavished upon me.
I am just so thankful to You, Lord,
for the cup of salvation I drink from daily
and for the healing You have performed in my life.
Amen.

For This Reason

DAY 58

Record one key reference each from your readings
in Mark and Psalms:

Turn your references into a prayer.

For This Reason

DAY 59

Scripture: Mark 9–16; Psalms 117 and 118

Heaven and earth shall pass away: but My words shall not pass away.
Mark 13:31

It is better to trust in the LORD than to put confidence in man. It is better to trust in the LORD than to put confidence in princes.
Psalm 118:8–9

*Unchanging Father,
the heavens will pass away and
the earth will be burned up,*
but Your Word will endure forever.
Your Word alone will stand the test of time,
and the forces of evil will not prevail against it.
Father, how foolish I am when
I put my trust in temporal and earthly aids.
How fickle the outcome of my life will be
if my dependence rests upon them.
You are unchanging and unwavering in
character and word, Father. Help me to wisely
invest in the incorruptible and eternal.
Amen.*

*2 Peter 3:10

For This Reason

DAY 59

Record one key reference each from your readings in Mark and Psalms:

Turn your references into a prayer.

For This Reason

DAY 60

Scripture: Ezekiel 1–12; Psalm 119:1–40

Now it came to pass in the thirtieth year, in the fourth month, in the fifth day of the month, as I was among the captives by the river of Chebar, that the heavens were opened, and I saw visions of God.

Ezekiel 1:1

Thy testimonies also are my delight and my counselors.

Psalm 119:24

*Liberating Father,
I'm so thankful for this passage that
identifies You as the source of hope
when I am in despair.
You chose to speak to Your servant Ezekiel
in a very bleak period of Israel's sinful history,
and You revealed Yourself to him in captivity.
Father, I need that same grace and vision in my life today,
even while facing the consequences of my sin.
Thank You for making Your grace available to me during
periods of captivity and for reminding me
that You love me and are not finished with me.
Let my heart be given over to Your testimonies,
and may Your word be a delight to my soul.
Amen.*

For This Reason

DAY 60

Record one key reference each from your readings in Ezekiel and Psalms.

Turn your references into a prayer.

For This Reason

DAY 61

Scripture: Ezekiel 13–24; Psalm 119:41–80

Son of man, these men have set up their idols in their heart, and put the stumblingblock of their iniquity before their face: should I be enquired of at all by them?
Ezekiel 14:3

I thought on my ways, and turned my feet unto Thy testimonies.
Psalm 119:59

*Pure Father,
Your love is pure and Your eyes are holy.
You avoid unnecessary use of the rod, but
when it is required You will apply it,
for my good and Your glory.
Sin mars my vision and disrupts
my communion with You;
thank You for the warnings in Your Word
that serve to protect and preserve my life.
Help me to respond obediently when You correct me,
and help me to see discipline as part of genuine love.
Bring to light any idol or stumbling block, Lord,
and cause my feet to stay on the pathway of righteousness.
Your love is pure and good; Your eyes are holy.
Amen.*

For This Reason

DAY 61

Record one key reference each from your readings in Ezekiel and Psalms:

Turn your references into a prayer.

DAY 62

Scripture: Ezekiel 25–36; Psalm 119:81–120

And ye My flock, the flock of My pasture, are men, and I am your God, saith the Lord GOD.

Ezekiel 34:31

Thou art my hiding place and my shield: I hope in Thy word.

Psalm 119:114

*Good Shepherd,
thank you for taking me into Your sheepfold
and making me one of Your own.
Thank you for placing me in a safe pasture
and giving me Your Word to feed on.
Thank you for claiming me as Your child
and for redeeming me with the blood of Your Son.
You have given me everything I need
for life and godliness and withheld nothing from me.
You are the Good Shepherd.
Your voice is familiar to me,
and Your Word is a comfort to me.
You pick me up and hold me when I am wounded,
and You hear my fearful cry when I have gone astray.
Give rest to my soul, and be my hiding place and shield.
Amen.*

For This Reason

DAY 62

Record one key reference each from your readings
in Ezekiel and Psalms:

Turn your references into a prayer.

For This Reason

DAY 63

Scripture: Ezekiel 37–48; Psalm 119:121–150

And they shall teach My people the difference between the holy and profane, and cause them to discern between the unclean and the clean.

Ezekiel 44:23

Order my steps in Thy word: and let not any iniquity have dominion over me.
Psalm 119:133

*Cleansing Father,
I am in this world, but I am not of this world.
The toxins and pollutants that surround me
serve to remind me that I am being preserved
and set apart for something far greater.
I am of the saints—holy, sacred, and distinctively
different from others. I bear a holy name, and a
holy name bears me. I am a pilgrim and sojourner
here on earth, with promises still awaiting fulfillment,
and eternal provision still to come.
This is praiseworthy, and fills my soul with rejoicing.
Order my steps according to Your Word,
and let no sin have dominion over me.
Let the manifestation of Your Spirit be evident to all,
and distinguish me as Your peculiar
and chosen possession.
Amen.*

For This Reason

DAY 63

Record one key reference each from your readings in Ezekiel and Psalms:

Turn your references into a prayer.

For This Reason

DAY 64

Scripture: Luke 1–12; Psalm 119:151–176

And, behold, thou shalt conceive in thy womb, and bring forth a son, and shalt call His name Jesus. He shall be great, and shall be called the Son of the Highest: and the Lord God shall give unto Him the throne of His father David: And He shall reign over the house of Jacob for ever; and of His kingdom there shall be no end.

Luke 1:31–33

Thy word is true from the beginning: and every one of Thy righteous judgments endureth for ever.

Psalm 119:160

*Redeeming Father,
the most precious story on earth begins
and ends with Jesus. When I consider this divine act of
redemptive love, everything in my life gives way to simple
praise and adoration of Your name.
You chose a perfect sacrifice to make atonement for me
and declared me righteous through Him.
You grant Him the supremacy of nations and kingdoms
and give Him authority to rule over all.
You have withheld nothing from Him, because He withheld
nothing from me. Jesus Christ is Lord.
Your Word is true from beginning to end,
and it will endure.
Amen.*

For This Reason

DAY 64

Record one key reference each from your readings in Luke and Psalms:

Turn your references into a prayer.

For This Reason

DAY 65

Scripture: Luke 13–24; Psalms 120 and 121

For whosoever shall be ashamed of Me and of My words, of him shall the Son of man be ashamed, when He shall come in His own glory, and in His Father's, and of the holy angels.
Luke 9:26

My help cometh from the Lord, which made heaven and earth.
Psalm 121:2

❦

Father, desire of my heart,
today I will be given opportunity
to speak about You to another.
Empower me to declare unashamedly my love for You.
Forgive me, Lord, when my spirit shrinks and
cowers from making known Your great Name.
There is no excuse. May it not be said of me
that I spoke little or poorly of You when You have
redeemed my very life! Ignite the same courage
within me that You gave to the saints and martyrs
of old—a testament to Your glory and a revelation
of Your Spirit's power. My help comes from You,
Lord, the Maker of heaven and earth.
Indwell me with Your hallmarks of
faith and courage.
Amen.

For This Reason

DAY 65

Record one key reference each from your readings
in Luke and Psalms:

Turn your references into a prayer.

For This Reason

DAY 66

Scripture: Daniel 1–12; Psalm 122–123

But Daniel purposed in his heart that he would not defile himself with the portion of the king's meat, nor with the wine which he drank: therefore he requested of the prince of the eunuchs that he might not defile himself.

Daniel 1:8

Behold, as the eyes of servants look unto the hand of their masters, and as the eyes of a maiden unto the hand of her mistress; so our eyes wait upon the Lord our God, until that He have mercy upon us.

Psalm 123:2

*Empowering Father,
Daniel was living in a land of captivity
and compromise, yet still his life was ruled
and settled by conviction. His communion with You
tempered his responses to the environment around him,
and he remained faithful to You in every arena of his life.
He was granted prestige, power, and position,
but what he prized was honoring and loving You.
O Father, make me a Daniel. Let my steps today
illustrate a steady walk with You, and let my decisions be
governed by the strength of Your Word.
My eyes look to you as a servant looks to his master.
Amen.*

For This Reason

DAY 66

Record one key reference each from your readings in Daniel and Psalms:

Turn your references into a prayer.

For This Reason

DAY 67

Scripture: John 1–10; Psalms 124 and 125

And I give unto them eternal life; and they shall never perish, neither shall any man pluck them out of My hand.

John 10:28

They that trust in the LORD shall be as mount Zion, which cannot be removed, but abideth for ever.

Psalm 125:1

*Eternal Father,
Your promises are based on Your faithful and
trustworthy character, and not one of them
will ever fail me.
Today You affirm to me the promise of
eternal life and abiding security—
the promise that nothing and no one
can snatch me from Your sovereign, almighty hand.
The promise that I am safe and secure in You.
Just as You have established Mount Zion
as Your eternal residence,
so have you secured me in Your everlasting love.
Your ways are infinite and good,
wonderful and unsearchable.
Amen.*

For This Reason

DAY 67

Record one key reference each from your readings in John and Psalms:

Turn your references into a prayer.

DAY 68

Scripture: John 11–21; Psalms 126 and 127

I am the vine, ye are the branches: He that abideth in Me, and I in him, the same bringeth forth much fruit: for without Me ye can do nothing.
John 15:5

He that goeth forth and weepeth, bearing precious seed, shall doubtless come again with rejoicing, bringing his sheaves with him.
Psalm 126:6

*Indwelling Father,
a magnificent promise is given to me
here in Your Word: Fruitfulness is synonymous
with Your faithfulness in my life—
fruit is the byproduct of abiding in You.
You have even determined beforehand
the productivity of my life: "much fruit."
I long to abide in You today, Lord, and be
a productive, fruitful branch for Your glory.
Regard my desire and feed me from the
life-giving vine of Your Word.
Let me bear Your precious seed
with a spirit of rejoicing,
bringing in the sheaves.
Amen.*

For This Reason

DAY 68

Record one key reference each from your readings in John and Psalms:

Turn your references into a prayer.

DAY 69

Scripture: Hosea 1–14; Psalms 128 and 129

Sow to yourselves in righteousness, reap in mercy; break up your fallow ground: for it is time to seek the LORD, till He come and rain righteousness upon you.

Hosea 10:12

Blessed is every one that feareth the LORD; that walketh in His ways.

Psalm 128:1

*Merciful Father,
to receive Your word, my heart needs to be
cleansed of fleshly thorns and weeds.
Bring to my mind this moment, Father,
any wrongdoing in my life.
As I confess my sins openly before You,
I ask You to be merciful to me and
rain Your grace upon me.
Break up the fallow ground of my heart
and let it be a healthy seedbed of Your word.
Plant the tender seeds of truth deeply in my soul
and let them take root today.
Allow me to enjoy the blessing that comes
from fearing Your name and walking in Your ways.
Let me sow in righteousness and reap in mercy.
Amen.*

For This Reason

DAY 69

Record one key reference each from your readings in Hosea and Psalms:

Turn your references into a prayer.

For This Reason

DAY 70

Scripture: Acts 1–14; Psalm 130

But Peter and John answered and said unto them, Whether it be right in the sight of God to hearken unto you more than unto God, judge ye. For we cannot but speak the things which we have seen and heard.

Acts 4:19–20

Lord, hear my voice: let thine ears be attentive to the voice of my supplications.

Psalm 130:2

Attentive Father,
the religious and devout leaders
commanded Peter and John to abstain
from proclaiming Your name. They refused!
Their mouths would not be still, and their lips
would not be silenced. You had rescued these men
from the dominion of darkness, and You have done
the same for me. The power that enabled Peter and John to
speak well of You indwells me also; let my lips not be silent
but bear steady testimony of You. Make my tongue bold to
share Your word. Be attentive to my voice,
and fulfill my supplication.
Amen.

For This Reason

DAY 70

Record one key reference each from your readings
in Acts and Psalms:

Turn your references into a prayer.

For This Reason

DAY 71

Scripture: Acts 15–28; Psalm 131

And at midnight Paul and Silas prayed, and sang praises unto God: and the prisoners heard them. And suddenly there was a great earthquake, so that the foundations of the prison were shaken: and immediately all the doors were opened, and every one's bands were loosed.

Acts 16:25–26

Lord, my heart is not haughty, nor mine eyes lofty: neither do I exercise myself in great matters, or in things too high for me.

Psalm 131:1

Responsive Father,
Paul and Silas did in the cell
what they did in the temple;
they praised You and prayed.
Their environment had changed dramatically,
but the state of their soul was maintained by Your Holy
Spirit, proving that You are not the God of certain hours
or certain places but a timeless and unchanging God
who can be relied upon in any and every situation.
Father, today I give You praise in the midst of my trial,
confident that my soul is being developed through it.
Train my spirit in humility and my soul in praise.
Amen.

For This Reason

Day 71

Record one key reference each from your readings in Acts and Psalms:

Turn your references into a prayer.

For This Reason

DAY 72

Scripture: Joel 1–3; Psalm 132

And I will restore to you the years that the locust hath eaten, the cankerworm, and the caterpiller, and the palmerworm, My great army which I sent among you. And ye shall eat in plenty, and be satisfied, and praise the name of the Lord your God, that hath dealt wondrously with you: and My people shall never be ashamed.

Joel 2:25–26

I will abundantly bless her provision: I will satisfy her poor with bread.

Psalm 132:15

*Renewing Father,
thank you for using the locust and worm
of trial to reveal to me something of
Your character and manifold power.
You are not absent from what You give me
nor unaware of what eats at the frailty of my soul.
You transform agents of destruction for my good,
and You use them to conform my soul to Yours.
Bless me with spiritual provision today
as I eat of Your Word,
and satisfy me with Your abundance.
Amen.*

For This Reason

Day 72

Record one key reference each from your readings in Joel and Psalms:

Turn your references into a prayer.

For This Reason

DAY 73

Scripture: Amos 1–9; Obadiah; Psalm 133

But let judgment run down as waters, and righteousness as a mighty stream.
Amos 5:24

Though thou exalt thyself as the eagle, and though thou set thy nest among the stars, thence will I bring thee down, saith the Lord.
Obadiah 1:4

Behold, how good and how pleasant it is for brethren to dwell together in unity!
Psalm 133:1

*Refreshing Father,
let waters of truth and judgment and
life-giving streams of righteousness
flow into my life today from the reservoir of Your Word.
Let streams of refreshment be poured out
on the dry, parched places of my soul.
Refresh me today where I'm weary.
Bring down areas of pride and replace them
with mercy, grace, and compassion.
Let my soul be a pure habitation for Your Spirit,
and let those who love Your name
find unity in Your presence. Amen.*

For This Reason

Day 73

Record one key reference each from your readings in Amos, Obadiah, and Psalms:

Turn your references into a prayer.

For This Reason

DAY 74

Scripture: Romans 1–8; Psalm 134

For I am not ashamed of the gospel of Christ: for it is the power of God unto salvation to every one that believeth; to the Jew first, and also to the Greek.

Romans 1:16

Behold, bless ye the Lord, all ye servants of the Lord, which by night stand in the house of the Lord.
Lift up your hands in the sanctuary, and bless the Lord.

Psalm 134:1–2

*Strengthening Father,
give me a platform to speak about You today,
Lord, and fill me in advance with Scriptures
that meet the needs of another.
Let Your Spirit's power be the agent
that directs my tongue, and let me
be bold in declaring Your name.
Let the fear of man be swallowed up by the strength of
Your Spirit, and let me not quench His presence.
I am Your beloved servant, created to bless Your name.
Morning and evening let me diligent to call on You,
and let my love for You be lavishly
and openly displayed,
just as Your love is toward me. Amen.*

For This Reason

Day 74

Record one key reference each from your readings
in Romans and Psalms:

Turn your references into a prayer.

For This Reason

DAY 75

Scripture: Romans 9–16; Psalm 135

For He saith to Moses, I will have mercy on whom I will have mercy, and I will have compassion on whom I will have compassion. So then it is not of him that willeth, nor of him that runneth, but of God that sheweth mercy.

Romans 9:15–16

Whatsoever the Lord pleased, that did He in heaven, and in earth, in the seas, and all deep places.

Psalm 135:6

Father, lover of my soul,
I find of particular comfort the reality
that no amount of "doing" on my part
can usher me into relationship with You.
I love You only because You first loved me.
You are the great initiator of my life,
and without You I would never call on
Your name, desire You, or pursue You.
What a wonder to be so wonderfully chosen by You!
Replace the fears of my limited knowledge and
understanding with a heightened awareness
of Your sovereignty. Let me rest in the
reality of Your infinite wisdom.
You do what You please in the heavens and the earth,
and I derive pleasure in Your ways. Amen.

For This Reason

Day 75

Record one key reference each from your readings in Romans and Psalms:

Turn your references into a prayer.

For This Reason

DAY 76

Scripture: Jonah 1–4; Micah 1–7; Psalm 136

And the word of the LORD came unto Jonah the second time, saying, Arise, go unto Nineveh, that great city, and preach unto it the preaching that I bid thee.
Jonah 3:1–2

He hath shewed thee, O man, what is good; and what doth the LORD require of thee, but to do justly, and to love mercy, and to walk humbly with thy God?
Micah 6:8

O give thanks unto the LORD; for He is good: for His mercy endureth for ever.
Psalm 136:1

*Patient and merciful Father,
what an incredible story of mercy today
from Your Word! Forgive me for the times
I have been less than gracious to other people,
and give me a second opportunity,
like Jonah's, to demonstrate
true mercy and compassion.
I long to do justly, love mercy,
and walk humbly with You. Amen.*

For This Reason

Day 76

Record one key reference each from your readings in Jonah, Micah, and Psalms:

Turn your references into a prayer.

For This Reason

DAY 77

Scripture: 1 Corinthians 1–8; Psalm 137

Now we have received, not the spirit of the world, but the spirit which is of God; that we might know the things that are freely given to us of God.

1 Corinthians 2:12

How shall we sing the Lord's song in a strange land?

Psalm 137:4

*Gracious Father,
You have anointed me and sealed me
with Your very Spirit that I might know
the things that have been freely given to me in You.
How utterly amazing it is that one third
of the eternal Godhead resides in me!
You have not left me alone in this world
but have chosen to indwell me
and to bring to life the truth of the Scriptures in me.
Because of Your Spirit, I am one with You.
Whether I find myself in a strange land or a familiar one,
still Your Spirit will remain with me.
Yes, I shall sing Your praises wherever You place me,
and Your Spirit shall go with me always.
Amen.*

For This Reason

Day 77

Record one key reference each from your readings
in 1 Corinthians and Psalms:

Turn your references into a prayer.

For This Reason

DAY 78

Scripture: 1 Corinthians 9–16; Psalm 138

There hath no temptation taken you but such as is common to man: but God is faithful, who will not suffer you to be tempted above that ye are able; but will with the temptation also make a way to escape, that ye may be able to bear it.

1 Corinthians 10:13

Though I walk in the midst of trouble, Thou wilt revive me: Thou shalt stretch forth Thine hand against the wrath of mine enemies, and Thy right hand shall save me.

Psalm 138:7

*Sufficient Father,
three times in this passage You refer to temptation,
and three times You promise to deliver me from it.
All temptations are opportunities for You
to manifest Your power in my life.
You will never leave me or forsake me.
Your faithfulness is sufficient in my every trial,
and Your Word is accessible to me daily.
Help me to make use of it and wield it against Satan's
lies and devices. Though I walk in the midst of trouble,
You will revive me, and Your right hand will surely create
my way of escape and deliver me.
Amen.*

For This Reason

Day 78

Record one key reference each from your readings
in 1 Corinthians and Psalms:

Turn your references into a prayer.

DAY 79

Scripture: 2 Corinthians 1–13; Psalm 139

While we look not at the things which are seen, but at the things which are not seen: for the things which are seen are temporal; but the things which are not seen are eternal.

2 Corinthians 4:18

If I say, Surely the darkness shall cover me; even the night shall be light about me. Yea, the darkness hideth not from Thee; but the night shineth as the day: the darkness and the light are both alike to Thee.

Psalm 139:11–12

*Radiant Father,
my afflictions never seem light or momentary,
and yet You tell me that, in light of eternity, they are.
Though I cannot always see how,
these trials help You show Your glory through my life.
Thank you that, no matter how dark
my troubles seem, even there You are with me.
Darkness and light are alike to You,
and the darkness cannot quench
the light of Your power and presence.
Amen.*

For This Reason

Day 79

Record one key reference each from your readings
in 2 Corinthians and Psalms:

Turn your references into a prayer.

For This Reason

DAY 80

Scripture: Nahum 1–3; Habakkuk 1–3; Zephaniah 1–3; Haggai 1–2; Psalm 140

The LORD is good, a strong hold in the day of trouble; and He knoweth them that trust in Him.

Nahum 1:7

Yet I will rejoice in the LORD, I will joy in the God of my salvation.

Habakkuk 3:18

Surely the righteous shall give thanks unto Thy name: the upright shall dwell in Thy presence.

Psalm 140:13

❦

Trustworthy Father,
my heart is heavy and my burdens weighty today.
How thankful I am for Your lovingkindness toward me and
for the place of refuge and strength that You afford.
When I am with You, troubles cease and peace enters in;
anxiety gives way to rejoicing, and joy swallows up sorrow.
In You I am made righteous and holy, and unto You
I offer thanksgiving and praise. You are my stronghold,
and I am made strong in You.
Amen.

For This Reason

Day 80

Record one key reference each from your readings in Nahum, Habakkuk, Zephaniah, Haggai, and Psalms:

Turn your references into a prayer.

For This Reason

DAY 81

***Scripture: 1 Thessalonians 1–5;
2 Thessalonians 1–3; Psalm 141***

And the very God of peace sanctify you wholly; and I pray God your whole spirit and soul and body be preserved blameless unto the coming of our Lord Jesus Christ.

1 Thessalonians 5:23

But the Lord is faithful, who shall stablish you, and keep you from evil.

2 Thessalonians 3:3

But mine eyes are unto Thee, O GOD the Lord: in Thee is my trust; leave not my soul destitute.

Psalm 141:8

*Sanctifying Father,
You have set me apart for noble purposes—
for the proclamation of Your gospel
and for the glory of Your name.
You will preserve every part of my being
until Your coming, and You will faithfully
establish me in every good word and work.
Keep me from evil, and thwart the advances of Satan intended to
diminish Your glory. My eyes are on You,
Lord, and my soul finds its rest in You alone.
Sanctify me wholly. Amen.*

For This Reason

Day 81

Record one key reference each from your readings in 1 Thessalonians, 2 Thessalonians, and Psalms:

Turn your references into a prayer.

For This Reason

DAY 82

Scripture: Zechariah 1–14; Psalm 142

And he shewed me Joshua the high priest standing before the angel of the Lord, and Satan standing at his right hand to resist him. And the Lord said unto Satan, The Lord rebuke thee, O Satan; even the Lord that hath chosen Jerusalem rebuke thee: is not this a brand plucked out of the fire?
Zechariah 3:1–2

Attend unto my cry; for I am brought very low: deliver me from my persecutors; for they are stronger than I.
Psalm 142:6

Father, my Defender,
how often it seems that Satan is standing near
as the oppressor and accuser of my soul—
waging war against me and reminding me
of my inadequacies, failures, and sins.
How overwhelmed I am at Your defense of me!
You are with me; You cover me with the
scarlet blood of Your Son, and I am made
white as snow, and sealed with Your name.
O Lord, when I am in the depths of despair
and brought low, please deliver, pardon, and rescue me.
You are my defender, My great High Priest.
Amen.

For This Reason

Day 82

Record one key reference each from your readings in Zechariah and Psalms:

Turn your references into a prayer.

For This Reason

DAY 83

Scripture: Malachi 1–4; Psalm 143

And they shall be Mine, saith the LORD of hosts, in that day when I make up My jewels; and I will spare them, as a man spareth his own son that serveth him. Then shall ye return, and discern between the righteous and the wicked, between him that serveth God and him that serveth Him not.
Malachi 3:17–18

Teach me to do Thy will; for Thou art my God: Thy Spirit is good; lead me into the land of uprightness.

Psalm 143:10

*Listening Father,
this passage never fails to inspire and stir me:
someone is recording the names and conversations
of those employed in speaking of You,
and each is being assigned in a book of remembrance.
How I long to see the recording of my name and
conversation in this special book, and
what a challenge that imposes on the
sharp little instrument of my tongue.
May I be known for lips that would not be silent for You.
Lead me by Your Spirit, and direct the course of my feet
and my tongue throughout this day.
Amen.*

For This Reason

Day 83

Record one key reference each from your readings
in Malachi and Psalms:

Turn your references into a prayer.

For This Reason

DAY 84

Scripture: 1 Timothy 1–6; 2 Timothy 1–4; Psalm 144

Which in His times He shall shew, who is the blessed and only Potentate, the King of kings, and Lord of lords; Who only hath immortality, dwelling in the light which no man can approach unto; whom no man hath seen, nor can see: to whom be honour and power everlasting. Amen.

1 Timothy 6:15–16

Happy is that people, that is in such a case: yea, happy is that people, whose God is the LORD.

Psalm 144:15

∽

Immortal Father,
Your glory exhausts all words, but still
I am drawn by this uncommon word potentate,*
describing You as a singular wielder
of authoritative power.
You are King of Kings, Lord of Lords, immortal,
adorned in light, unapproachable in holiness,
and with power everlasting.
Should I not rejoice that such a God is my God?
Blessed and only Potentate, You are gloriously God.

* *Potent* means "strong and powerful"; *potentate* means "wielding a strong authority" (*Webster's Seventh New Collegiate Dictionary*, G. & C. Merriam Company, 1965).

For This Reason

Day 84

Record one key reference each from your readings in 1 Timothy, 2 Timothy, and Psalms:

Turn your references into a prayer.

DAY 85

Scripture: Titus 1–3; Philemon; Psalm 145

Looking for that blessed hope, and the glorious appearing of the great God and our Saviour Jesus Christ; who gave Himself for us, that He might redeem us from all iniquity, and purify unto Himself a peculiar people, zealous of good works.

Titus 2:13–14

Every day will I bless Thee; and I will praise Thy name for ever and ever. Great is the Lord, and greatly to be praised; and His greatness is unsearchable.

Psalm 145:2–3

Trustworthy Father,
I look expectantly for Your return, and I know
that the word You have spoken is
the word You will perform.
Your first coming signaled my redemption,
and Your second coming signals my release,
when at last I will be with You.
As Your peculiar possession, I am to be proclaiming
Your name and performing Your work until You come.
Fill me with holy zeal for the tasks You have appointed
for me. Let blessing spring forth from my lips
and let praise be constantly on my tongue.
Unsearchable are Your ways, and indescribable Your glory.
Amen.

For This Reason

Day 85

Record one key reference each from your readings in Titus, Philemon, and Psalms:

Turn your references into a prayer.

DAY 86

Scripture: Hebrews 1–13; Psalm 146

Wherefore seeing we also are compassed about with so great a cloud of witnesses, let us lay aside every weight, and the sin which doth so easily beset us, and let us run with patience the race that is set before us, looking unto Jesus the author and finisher of our faith; who for the joy that was set before Him endured the cross, despising the shame, and is set down at the right hand of the throne of God.
Hebrews 12:1–2

Happy is he that hath the God of Jacob for his help, whose hope is in the Lord his God:
Psalm 146:5

*Encompassing Father,
it delights me to think of the host of
witnesses who encompass my life:
Abraham, Moses, Joseph, Deborah, David, Daniel, Ezra...
Each of these people fulfilled a part of Your plan
and left me a treasury of testimony
about Your character and Your faithfulness.
Let my race be clean, swift, and without the
weight of besetting sins, focused on Jesus and
dependent upon the God of Jacob.
Amen.*

For This Reason

Day 86

Record one key reference each from your readings in Hebrews and Psalms:

Turn your references into a prayer.

For This Reason

DAY 87

Scripture: James 1–5; 1 Peter 1–5; 2 Peter 1–3; Psalm 147

Be ye also patient; stablish your hearts: for the coming of the Lord draweth nigh.
James 5:8

But the end of all things is at hand: be ye therefore sober, and watch unto prayer.
1 Peter 4:7

Great is our Lord, and of great power: His understanding is infinite.
Psalm 147:5

*Eternal Father,
there will come a day when the patient,
wise, and persevering will see Your face.
This time on earth is so brief, and yet so much of my
response toward You is tangled up in earthly things.
The end is near, and I must live like it.
Keep me purposeful in my proclamation of the gospel,
and make me sober and watchful to the end.
Help me to redeem the time, because the days are evil,
and make me faithful in prayer and communion with You.
Your glory and power are great and limitless,
and Your understanding is infinite.
How excellent Your return will be!
Amen.*

For This Reason

Day 87

Record one reference each from your readings in James, 1 & 2 Peter, and Psalms:

Turn your references into a prayer.

For This Reason

DAY 88

Scripture: 1 John 1–5; 2 John; 3 John; Jude; Psalm 148

But the anointing which ye have received of Him abideth in you, and ye need not that any man teach you: but as the same anointing teacheth you of all things, and is truth, and is no lie, and even as it hath taught you, ye shall abide in Him.

1 John 2:27

Praise ye the Lord. Praise ye the Lord from the heavens: praise Him in the heights.

Psalm 148:1

*Father, my Teacher,
there are countless resources to aid me
in my knowledge of You, and a thousand works
of gifted men to ponder, but only one will stand the test of
time and be effective in changing my heart:
the written Word of God. There are a thousand
brilliant teachers, but only One who can accurately testify
to the truths contained in Your Word: the Holy Spirit.
When the Word of God and the Spirit of God collide in me,
their impact is glorious, and their discerning
immeasurable. Praise to You, Lord,
for Your infinite wisdom and ways.
Amen.*

For This Reason

Day 88

Record one key reference each from your readings in 1 John, 2 John, 3 John, Jude, and Psalms:

Turn your references into a prayer.

For This Reason

DAY 89

Scripture: Revelation 1–11; Psalm 149

I am Alpha and Omega, the beginning and the ending, saith the Lord, which is, and which was, and which is to come, the Almighty.
Revelation 1:8

Praise ye the LORD. Sing unto the LORD a new song, and His praise in the congregation of saints.
Psalm 149:1

*Everlasting Father,
You save the best for the last,
and usher in an astonishing disclosure of Your Son,
Jesus Christ, in Your final letter.
The intent seems clear:
To afford me an early understanding of Him
before His return, and to provide a
small glimpse of His glory.
I must be prepared, watching, and waiting,
because the time is drawing near.
The one thing on earth worth waiting for is You.
I praise You, Lord, and lift up my voice in adoration.
I believe that every word You've given is true.
Amen.*

For This Reason

Day 89

Record one key reference each from your readings
in Revelation and Psalms:

Turn your references into a prayer.

For This Reason

DAY 90

Scripture: Revelation 12–22; Psalm 150

And the Spirit and the bride say, Come. And let him that heareth say, Come. And let him that is athirst come. And whosoever will, let him take the water of life freely.

Revelation 22:17

He which testifieth these things saith, Surely I come quickly. Amen. Even so, come, Lord Jesus.
The grace of our Lord Jesus Christ be with you all. Amen.

Revelation 22:20–21

Let every thing that hath breath praise the Lord. Praise ye the Lord.

Psalm 150:6

*Perfect Father,
how fitting that Your final words to me
are a testimony about what You have in store for me
and what You've made available to me through Christ.
I gladly accept Your invitation!
Freely I come, freely I drink, and freely You give to me.
Nothing has been withheld from me;
You have loved me with an everlasting love.
Come soon, Lord Jesus,
and let my final breath be drawn in You.
Amen.*

For This Reason

Day 90

Record one key reference each from your readings in Revelation and Psalms:

Turn your references into a prayer.

Notes